A Believer's
Companion

A Believer's Companion

Noleen Herbert

A BELIEVER'S COMPANION
Copyright © 2023 by Noleen Herbert

All rights reserved. Neither this publication nor any part of this publication may be reproduced or transmitted in any form or by any means, electronic or mechanical, including photocopying, recording or any information storage and retrieval system, without permission in writing from the author.

Scripture quotations taken from the Amplified® Bible (AMP), Copyright © 2015 by The Lockman Foundation. Used by permission. lockman.org Scripture quotations marked (NLT) are taken from the Holy Bible, New Living Translation, copyright ©1996, 2004, 2015 by Tyndale House Foundation. Used by permission of Tyndale House Publishers, Carol Stream, Illinois 60188. All rights reserved. Scripture quotations marked (KJV) taken from the Holy Bible, King James Version, which is in the public domain. Scripture quotations are from the ESV® Bible (The Holy Bible, English Standard Version®), copyright © 2001 by Crossway, a publishing ministry of Good News Publishers. Used by permission. All rights reserved. The ESV text may not be quoted in any publication made available to the public by a Creative Commons license. The ESV may not be translated in whole or in part into any other language. Scripture quotations marked MSG are taken from The Message, copyright © 1993, 2002, 2018 by Eugene H. Peterson. Used by permission of NavPress. All rights reserved. Represented by Tyndale House Publishers.

ISBN: 978-1-4866-2437-9
eBook ISBN: 978-1-4866-2438-6

Word Alive Press
119 De Baets Street Winnipeg, MB R2J 3R9
www.wordalivepress.ca

Cataloguing in Publication information can be obtained from Library and Archives Canada.

Many thanks to all the pastors, apostles, evangelists, and bishops I have come across throughout my Christian journey. Thanks also to my husband and friend, Herbert, and my two children, Jaden and Ayana. Finally, I thank the Lord Jesus Christ, who revealed himself to me.

Contents

Introduction		ix
One	SALVATION	1
Two	BAPTISM	7
Three	BIBLE STUDY	11
Four	FRIENDSHIP WITH THE HOLY SPIRIT	19
Five	CONSECRATION	21
Six	PRAYER	27
Seven	DELIVERANCE	37
Eight	SELECTING A LOCAL CHURCH	41
Appendix	PRAYERS AND DECLARATIONS	43

Introduction

I have been a believer for decades, and during my journey I went around in circles discovering Jesus Christ and what he did on the cross. No one was there to really sit me down and teach me the basics. Christian faith was about giving my life to Christ so I wouldn't go to hell, then joining a church. After getting saved, I felt like a zoo animal being thrown into the wild.

I later discovered that I wasn't the only one. Many Christians out there are either living in total ignorance or only understanding half-truths. This is very dangerous. When persecution comes, you won't remain resolute if you aren't strongly rooted in your belief system. Also, you may feed others the same poison. Before you know it, the whole body is sick.

On the day when Jesus comes back, he may find no one left standing. He could end up like Noah, who only saved animals.

Would we want that to be our portion? Absolutely not.

As you go through this book, you will come to understand all the basics of Christian faith—and in simple language. I know you're going to be edified, be blessed, and develop a strong foundation in Christ Jesus. Amen!

One
SALVATION

Salvation is the greatest gift of God to humanity. He foresaw before the foundation of the world that we were going to fail him through sin. He also knew that we would need a redeemer to deliver us from the tentacles of sins, transgressions, iniquities, and abominations.

Sin is an offence against a religious rule that causes division or fights. Others may even follow suit or become discouraged. Sin is a fault in humanity that sets us apart from God because of our fleshly bodies.

A transgression is a violation or breaking of the law. During the time of Moses, the people followed the Ten Commandments. So if one were to covet another man's wife, despite the commandment that says otherwise, that person would be counted as having committed a transgression.

> *Because the law worketh wrath: for where no law is, there is no transgression.* (Romans 4:15, KJV)

An iniquity is failing to do what you are expected to do. For example, David killed Uriah to take his wife Bathsheba. Nobody would have expected him to do this, but he went ahead and did it anyway. An iniquity is something done, or not done, by one person to another.

> *I acknowledge my sin unto thee, and mine iniquity have I not hid. I said, I will confess my transgressions unto the Lord; and thou forgavest the iniquity of my sin. Selah.* (Psalm 32:5, KJV)

An abomination is something exceptionally loathsome, shameful, and treated with disgust—such as idolatry, the worshipping of other gods, homosexuality, murder, rape, etc.

ONE: SALVATION

> *These six things the Lord hates; indeed, seven are repulsive to Him: a proud look [the attitude that makes one overestimate oneself and discount others], a lying tongue, and hands that shed innocent blood, a heart that creates wicked plans, feet that run swiftly to evil, a false witness who breathes out lies [even half-truths], and one who spreads discord (rumors) among brothers.* (Proverbs 6:16–19, AMP)

God is a holy God. There is no filth or defilement in him. To approach and commune with him, one needs to be clean. So when men first came into existence, they failed God through the disobedience of Adam and Eve in the garden of Eden. They chose to listen to the devil rather than follow the instructions of God. Because of that, men were separated from God. That was the beginning of sin.

Later, God ushered in the Ten Commandments to Moses so that men could know what is wrong and what is right. However, as men followed the law, it was clear that it empowered sin, such that it became worse than before. So the main solution was for Jesus to come and clean human sin with his blood.

1.1 Salvation through Works

The concept of receiving salvation through works came to us through the Law of Moses. During this period, the people would clean their sins by sacrificing animals. The blood was used to make the people righteous again before God.

The blood of animals didn't bestow perfection, however, as people were required to make sacrifices over and over to be cleansed from their sins. For example, if you committed adultery, you would sacrifice an animal. If you stole a goat the next day, you would need to make another sacrifice to be cleansed.

Glory be to God, who chose a better way for us. That better way is the concept of receiving salvation instead through faith.

1.2 Salvation through Faith

Salvation through faith was God's trump card for dealing with the issue of sin. In this way, sin was defeated once and for all.

All we have to do now is believe in his only begotten son, Jesus, and believe that God sent him to be the ultimate sacrificial lamb to bring reconciliation between men and God. There is no longer a need to sacrifice anything for the remission of sin. Jesus's blood has cleansed all sin, past and present, until judgment day. What a good God we have!

Two
Baptism

After giving our lives to Jesus, we must follow the practices of New Testament Christians, who were baptized first in water and then the Spirit as a sign of Jesus's death, burial, and resurrection.

2.1 Baptism through Water

The whole body was immersed in water to signify, as written, the burial of the old man of sin. It also signifies the act of being cleansed of past abominations.

As a person is taken out of the water, that represents being resurrected to a new life in Jesus Christ and being translated from the kingdom of darkness to the kingdom of light.

> *Or are you ignorant of the fact that all of us who have been baptized into Christ Jesus were baptized into His death? We have therefore been buried with Him through baptism into death, so that just as Christ was raised from the dead through the glory and power of the Father, we too might walk habitually in newness of life [abandoning our old ways]. For if we have become one with Him [permanently united] in the likeness of His death, we will also certainly be [one with Him and share fully] in the likeness of His resurrection. We know that our old self [our human nature without the Holy Spirit] was nailed to the cross with Him, in order that our body of sin might be done away with, so that we would no longer be slaves to sin. For the person who has died [with Christ] has been freed from [the power of] sin.* (Romans 6:3–7, AMP)

After being baptized in water, we can publicly proclaim we are believers. All has passed away and we are new creations in Christ Jesus.

2.2 Baptism of the Holy Spirit

The most important step after water baptism is being baptized in the Holy Spirit. This is a seal of God upon our spirit man to say that we have indeed been born of God.

> *In Him, you also, when you heard the word of truth, the good news of your salvation, and [as a result] believed in Him, were stamped with the seal of the promised Holy Spirit [the One promised by Christ] as owned and protected [by God].* (Ephesians 1:13, AMP)

The Holy Spirit then comes in and dwell inside us, together with our own spirit, and begins to operate inside-out as we feed him with the word of God.

2.3 Baptism by Fire

This is when the Holy Spirit will come upon us. Being baptized by fire equips us for service. In Acts 2, the disciples awaited the first baptism:

> *And now, Lord, observe their threats [take them into account] and grant that Your bond-servants may declare Your message [of salvation] with great confidence, while*

> *You extend Your hand to heal, and signs and wonders (attesting miracles) take place through the name [and the authority and power] of Your holy Servant and Son Jesus." And when they had prayed, the place where they were meeting together was shaken [a sign of God's presence]; and they were all filled with the Holy Spirit and began to speak the word of God with boldness and courage.*
> (Acts 4:29–31, AMP)

Soon after the first baptism, another baptism came upon them and they began to perform miracles, signs, and wonders with confidence. They were equipped for service so they could preach the kingdom of God with power.

Three
BIBLE STUDY

The Bible isn't just a book with many stories or words. Behind those stories and words is power. The Bible is not the word of God, but it talks about the word of God.

> *In the beginning [before all time] was the Word (Christ), and the Word was with God, and the Word was God Himself.* (John 1:1, AMP)

Jesus is the word of God, and to know him we must read the Bible. The Bible was written under the inspiration of the Holy Spirit and there is no error in it. If it seems like there are some mistakes, that just means you haven't yet figured everything out. The more you study the word, the more you begin to understand who Jesus is. The more we search for him, the more we will get acquainted with him.

> *Then [with a deep longing] you will seek Me and require Me [as a vital necessity] and [you will] find Me when you search for Me with all your heart.* (Jeremiah 29:13, AMP)

We should study the Bible with Jesus in mind. Then we will see him manifesting both in the New and Old Testaments. He was hidden in the Old Testament, and in the New Testament he is revealed.

3.1 MEDITATION

We should not study the Bible as if it were a fiction book. I would agree that some stories in it are quite catchy, but every story contains a lesson that applies to our current situation. The Bible was written to serve as our example, so **be** **i**nformed **b**efore you **l**eave **e**arth.

Meditation is like chewing food. By chewing, we learn the flavors that make up the meal. In meditation, we must know who said something, why he or she said it, and to whom it was meant. And finally, are there any lessons to be taken from it? As we do this, we begin to receive revelation, causing mysteries in the word to be demystified.

It is important to not connect two different verses that have no relationship to each other. We also need to read and interpret verses in their original context—for example, reading the entire chapter they appear in—or else we may interpret them the wrong way.

For example, Acts 15:5 says,

> *But some from the sect of the Pharisees who had believed [in Jesus as the Messiah] stood up and said, "It is necessary to circumcise the Gentile converts and to direct them to observe the Law of Moses."* (AMP)

If you take this verse out of context, it may seem as though the practice of circumcision and the Law of Moses are still valid for New Testament Christians. They are not.

3.2 OLD TESTAMENT

Jesus appeared in the Old Testament as Melchizedek, the King of Salem. Then his death and resurrection can be seen in the story of Jonah. Christ even mentioned that no sign would be given to the generation in which he lived other than the sign of Jonah. He was talking about his death, burial, resurrection, and eventual ascension.

When God told Jonah to deliver Nineveh, Jonah cried out. This represented the Law, under which people were judged for sin—yet God showed mercy. Nineveh was forgiven after God promised its destruction.

Jonah's issue was all about the Law versus grace. The Law said that Nineveh wasn't qualified, but grace said that God could qualify the people if they repented. The Law had a temper tantrum. The Law spoke judgment, whereas grace spoke forgiveness.

The Law knew that it was the root cause of sin, yet it lay asleep, quietly wreaking havoc. Jonah slept in the boat, yet he was the root cause of everything. The Law isn't happy when a person is pardoned, for the Law speaks blood and judgment; grace speaks of love, mercy, and forgiveness.

So we realize here that the Old Testament's stories have a hidden, deeper meaning. All the stories since Abraham have pointed us to Jesus Christ.

The Old Testament also shows us how God dealt with men. There are many lessons to be learned from it. All the physical wars in the Old Testament represent spiritual wars with Satan in the New Testament.

We must also note that the Law of Moses, or the

Mosaic Law, was cancelled and nullified by the death of Jesus Christ. We do not have to follow the Law anymore. But then, you may say, Jesus said in the New Testament, *"I did not come to abolish the law of Moses or the writings of the prophets. No, I came to accomplish their purpose"* (Matthew 5:17, NLT).

The New Testament came into effect on the cross by Jesus's death. So the new covenant begins in the book of Acts by the coming in of the Holy Spirit. All who follow Jesus are under the Holy Spirit and should not follow anything having to do with the Law. The Law was abolished for all who believe in Christ, as Hebrews 8:13 says:

> *When God speaks of "A new covenant," He makes the first one obsolete. And whatever is becoming obsolete (out of use, annulled) and growing old is ready to disappear.* (AMP)

Those who follow the Law shall be judged according to the Law. The current church makes the mistake of mixing the two. Paul addressed this by saying,

> *It was for this freedom that Christ set us free [completely liberating us]; therefore keep*

> *standing firm and do not be subject again to a yoke of slavery [which you once removed].*
>
> *Notice, it is I, Paul, who tells you that if you receive circumcision [as a supposed requirement of salvation], Christ will be of no benefit to you [for you will lack the faith in Christ that is necessary for salvation]. Once more I solemnly affirm to every man who receives circumcision [as a supposed requirement of salvation], that he is under obligation and required to keep the whole Law. You have been severed from Christ, if you seek to be justified [that is, declared free of the guilt of sin and its penalty, and placed in right standing with God] through the Law; you have fallen from grace [for you have lost your grasp on God's unmerited favor and blessing]. For we [not relying on the Law but] through the [strength and power of the Holy] Spirit, by faith, are waiting [confidently] for the hope of righteousness [the completion of our salvation].* (Galatians 5:1–5, AMP)

When you follow one, you automatically forfeit the other. It is better to follow grace; that is where power is.

> *But [in fact] their minds were hardened [for they had lost the ability to understand]; for until this very day at the reading of the old covenant the same veil remains unlifted, because it is removed [only] in Christ. But to this day whenever Moses is read, a veil [of blindness] lies over their heart; but whenever a person turns [in repentance and faith] to the Lord, the veil is taken away.* (2 Corinthians 3:14–16, AMP)

Added to this, if we follow the Law of Moses, we are separated from the glory of God and become totally lost.

3.3 New Testament

The New Testament begins after the death, burial, resurrection, and ascension of Jesus Christ. Christ gave birth to us on the cross and, according to Colossians 2:14–15, cancelled everything that was against us. He not only did that, but he also dealt with principalities, powers, rulers of darkness, and spiritual wickedness in high places.

As New Testament Christians, we are fighting wars with a defeated enemy. We are confronting him from the point of victory, a platform of power, and a place of advantage. If we are ignorant of this fact, the devil will take advantage of our ignorance. That is why it is written, *"Lest Satan should get an advantage of us: for we are not ignorant of his devices"* (2 Corinthians 2:11, KJV).

We should also spend more effort trying to understand the epistles of Paul. They both remind us of the power we have and demystify Jesus Christ's reality. Without Christ, there is no church.

Four
FRIENDSHIP WITH THE HOLY SPIRIT

We read in John 14:26,

> *But the Helper (Comforter, Advocate, Intercessor—Counselor, Strengthener, Standby), the Holy Spirit, whom the Father will send in My name [in My place, to represent Me and act on My behalf], He will teach you all things. And He will help you remember everything that I have told you.* (AMP)

As we can see here, the Holy Spirit accomplishes so much in our journeys with Christ. Without him, our lives would not have the impact expected of us as children of God. When we go through deep waters and face the troubles of life, he will raise the standard against the enemy for our comfort. When Satan rises to accuse us of the things we have or have not done, he is vindicates us. When we don't know how to pray and are praying amiss, because we lack understanding, he intercedes for us. When we don't know what to do, he gives us direction. When the challenges of life are overwhelming and we are consumed by confusion, he gives us good counsel. When we are tired and about to give up, he strengthens our resolve. He will always be by our side.

The Holy Spirit also helps us to grow into spiritual maturity. As we yield to him, we begin to grow fruit—the fruit of the spirit. Just as a tree grows into maturity, if it is healthy it will produce fruit. The fruit of the Holy Spirit is a sign that the Spirit of God is alive in us, and these are love, joy, kindness, peace, patience, generosity, self-control, gentleness, and faithfulness.

Five
CONSECRATION

In the Bible, consecration is the separation of oneself from that which is unclean, especially anything that would contaminate one's relationship with a perfect God. Consecration means removing yourself from the throne of your life and enthroning Jesus. It is walking according to the dictates of the Spirit and not the self. It is giving God absolute authority over your life.

We must remember that we were given free will to choose whom to follow in our lives. In the end, we will be judged on how we used that free will.

Consecration is about having an absolute love for God, trusting him, and obeying him. It is not a one-time decision. We will never reach perfection, but we should still strive toward it.

Living consecrated lives is a personal choice through which you constantly remind yourself and reflect on your motives. It is a kingdom-oriented life.

We live in this world but are not part of it. The world is not in us. The world is dark, but we are the light of the world. Our kingdom is not of this world but rather of the world to come.

This world in which we live is temporary and short; our future world is permanent. We should not forfeit the eternal for the immediate. We should embrace the good and reject the bad.

We should also have a conscious understanding that the enemy may offer you something good to trap you. That's why we need to walk in the Spirit. As 2 Corinthians 6:17 says, *"Therefore go out from their midst, and be separate from them, says the Lord, and touch no unclean thing; then I will welcome you…"* (ESV)

5.1 Overcoming Enemies to Consecration

Lust. We read in 1 John 2:16–17,

FIVE: CONSECRATION

> *For all that is in the world—the desires of the flesh and the desires of the eyes and pride of life—is not from the Father but is from the world. And the world is passing away along with its desires, but whoever does the will of God abides forever.* (ESV)

The desires of the flesh can be seen in behaviors that lead to adultery, fornication, and homosexuality. The desires of the eyes are temptations to look upon things we should not look upon. The pride of life is lusting after anything of the world that leads to arrogance; for example, personal achievements.

Jealousy. This spirit is gripping and I sometimes think we are born with it.

There was an occasion when my son and my niece spent the day with me. When I carried one of them, the other would cry. Everything I had to do that day, I had to do it for both. They also fought over toys.

The spirit of jealousy says, "I should be the one and not you." It is driven by competition.

We should bless others and congratulate others when they are blessed, because the same God who has done it for them is the one who will do it for us.

This spirit can easily operate in our lives, even in the body of Christ, and it can quench the move of the Spirit. This can be seen in the biblical examples of Jesus with his disciples and of Paul.

Mark 9:38–40 says,

> *John said to him, "Teacher, we saw someone casting out demons in your name, and we tried to stop him, because he was not following us." But Jesus said, "Do not stop him, for no one who does a mighty work in my name will be able soon afterward to speak evil of me. For the one who is not against us is for us."* (ESV)

Philippians 1:15–18 says,

> *It's true that some are preaching out of jealousy and rivalry. But others preach about Christ with pure motives. They preach because they love me, for they know I have been appointed to defend the Good News. Those others do not have pure motives as they preach about Christ. They preach with selfish ambition, not sincerely, intending to make my chains*

more painful to me. But that doesn't matter. Whether their motives are false or genuine, the message about Christ is being preached either way, so I rejoice. And I will continue to rejoice. (NLT)

In church, sometimes people fail to manifest their spiritual gifts because of jealousy, yet God has anointed them with these gifts for the benefit of the body of Christ.

Unforgiveness and bitterness. We all have people who love us, and sometimes we feel as though they love us more than we love ourselves. They know what's good for us, the person we should marry, and the choices that will be best for us. Sometimes having such people in our lives can be a pain.

The word of God says that we should forgive. However, we don't have to wait for the pain to leave in order for us to be able to forgive. Forgive while you are still hurting. That will give the Holy Spirit a starting point to work in us. He is the only one who can heal internal wounds. We may remember it afterward, but with time it will be nothing but a memory and the pain will be gone.

Pride. Pride is deadly because we sometimes aren't aware that we are walking in it. People with pride want everyone to bow to them; they are servants to no one.

They don't want anybody to teach them, since they already know everything. They have built walls such that they only allow certain people close to them; for example, the rich and popular. They look down on others.

Pride is the reason that Satan was chucked out of heaven. Pride resists spiritual giftings. People with pride struggle to walk or get baptized in the Holy Spirit because they are overly involved in the flesh.

We can only overcome pride by meditating on the word of God daily and being conscious of our actions.

Hate. We cannot say that we love God and hate his people. It is easy to love those who love us, but real love means loving those who don't love us back. We should pray for them and believe that one day the mercy of God will visit them.

You may notice that all these sins cannot be seen by the naked eye, but God can see them. They delay our spiritual growth.

Six
Prayer

Prayer is our power source. Jst like we charge our phones, prayer is how we charge our spirit man. We acquire power over the enemy through prayer. We pray together with others and are also encouraged to pray when we're alone in our secret place.

There are different kinds of prayers, including the prayer of faith, the prayer of groaning, the prayer of lamentation, and meditations of the heart. However, I am going to talk about the two types of prayer I have found to be most effective, especially for new believers: the prayer of faith and the prayer of groaning.

6.1 Prayer of Faith

We often emphasize the prayer of faith, because we received our salvation through faith. This type of prayer is when you pray by the word of God. We quote scriptures and bring them before God, because as he said, *"I am watching over my word to perform it"* (Jeremiah 1:12, ESV). God also said that he has exalted his word above his name (Psalm 138:2).

We can also add fasting to the prayer of faith, for Jesus said, *"Howbeit this kind goeth not out but by prayer and fasting"* (Matthew 17:21, KJV). So there is a kind of situation or problem that goes by prayer only and another that requires prayer and fasting. We can use the prayer of faith when we make declarations upon our lives, such as the things we want to see, and rebuking or rejecting the things we do not want to see.

6.2 Prayer of Groaning

There are prayers we can engage in as new believers, intercessors, parents, and children of God when it seems as though everything has failed, when something is not moving, when you want to cry for repentance for a wicked people, when you want to cry out for a sinful partner, when you want to cry out for souls, when you are in witchcraft bondage, when you are in captivity, when you are facing an evil pattern, when you are facing death, and when you are facing the beast of Ephesus. When your faith in God is limited or is failing, this is the right prayer.

Many will say, "I have done everything, but God is not answering." This is because they only know the prayer of faith.

Let me mention something that happened to me many years ago. While attending a concert, I began to talk about the groanings of the Spirit. Another sister overheard me and confessed that she had had three miscarriages and was carrying her fourth pregnancy. She told me that she had a dream each time she was pregnant, and every time the dream occurred, no matter the amount of prayer and fasting, she miscarried. She explained that she'd had this evil dream a few days before and was already feeling discouraged.

I taught her about praying through groaning by the Holy Spirit. Right there in the concert, she began to groan in the Holy Spirit and was totally delivered. She went on to deliver a baby boy.

Groaning in the Spirit is a prayer of being vulnerable to God. Groaning means having righteous anger, a certain anger against problems, and a certain disrespect towards the devil. This is a cry from one's loins without words, and it is a product of deeper love.

God is love and will move because he cannot deny himself. Groaning reminds God of the pain Jesus went through on the cross. He groaned and cried, *"My God, my God, why hast thou forsaken me?"* (Psalm 22:1) And God could not do anything.

When you groan, he remembers the cry of his Son dying for you and comes to your rescue.

Groaning is an expression of pain that goes beyond physical feelings. It is associated with child labor, because you want to bring out something. Psalms 5:1 says, *"Listen to my words, O Lord, consider my groaning and sighing"* (AMP). This was written by David, the friend of God. He would pray in words and then groan. Psalms 102:4–6 says,

> *My heart has been struck like grass and withered, indeed, [absorbed by my heartache] I forget to eat my food. Because of the sound of my groaning [in suffering and trouble] my bones cling to my flesh. I am like a [mournful] vulture of the wilderness; I am like a [desolate] owl of the wasteland.*
> (AMP)

The word groaning describes exactly how you feel. Whether you're justified or not, groaning is the answer.

Even when you have sown evil seed and must harvest it, mercy will show up when you groan. Psalm 102:19–20 says,

> *Tell them the Lord looked down from his heavenly sanctuary. He looked down to earth from heaven to hear the groans of the prisoners, to release those condemned to die.* (NLT)

When we are facing death in any area of our lives, we should groan in the Spirit.

> *Years passed, and the king of Egypt died. But the Israelites continued to groan under their burden of slavery. They cried out for help, and their cry rose up to God. God heard their groaning, and he remembered his covenant promise to Abraham, Isaac, and Jacob. He looked down on the people of Israel and knew it was time to act.* (Exodus 2:23–25, NLT)

When you want to come out of spiritual slavery, groan. God extended compassion and moved when he heard the groanings of Israel. He didn't act because of their fasting or complaining.

> *When Jesus therefore saw her weeping, and the Jews also weeping which came with her, he groaned in the spirit, and was troubled.*
>
> *And said, Where have ye laid him? They said unto him, Lord, come and see.*
>
> *Jesus wept.*
>
> *Then said the Jews, Behold how he loved him! And some of them said, Could not this man, which opened the eyes of the blind, have caused that even this man should not have died?*
>
> *Jesus therefore again groaning in himself cometh to the grave. It was a cave, and a stone lay upon it.* (John 11:33–38, KJV)

Groaning raises the dead. Lazarus came out of the grave because of the groanings of Jesus Christ. Miracles are a product of groanings.

> *Meanwhile, the moment we get tired in the waiting, God's Spirit is right alongside helping us along. If we don't know how or*

what to pray, it doesn't matter. He does our praying in and for us, making prayer out of our wordless sighs, our aching groans. He knows us far better than we know ourselves, knows our pregnant condition, and keeps us present before God. That's why we can be so sure that every detail in our lives of love for God is worked into something good. (Romans 8:26–28, MSG)

Another version of the same verse reads,

In the same way the Spirit [comes to us and] helps us in our weakness. We do not know what prayer to offer or how to offer it as we should, but the Spirit Himself [knows our need and at the right time] intercedes on our behalf with sighs and groanings too deep for words. And He who searches the hearts knows what the mind of the Spirit is, because the Spirit intercedes [before God] on behalf of God's people in accordance with God's will. (Romans 8:26–27, AMP)

By groaning, the Holy Spirit and your spirit come into unity and there is no need to interpret what you say or how you feel. You and the Holy Spirit will be praying together in one accord.

This also means that you are in unity with God himself. Groaning is a direct line to Yahweh. Every time you groan, God says something—one hundred percent of the time. There is no prince of Persia to hold your prayers, like what happened to Daniel in Daniel 10. Groanings destroy all protocols. The Holy Spirit is the only one who can tell the Father exactly how you feel on your behalf.

> *O come, let us sing joyfully to the Lord; let us shout joyfully to the rock of our salvation. Let us come before His presence with a song of thanksgiving; let us shout joyfully to Him with songs. For the Lord is a great God and a great King above all gods, in whose hand are the depths of the earth; the peaks of the mountains are His also. The sea is His, for He made it [by His command]; and His hands formed the dry land. O come, let us worship and bow down, let us kneel before the Lord our Maker [in reverent praise and prayer].* (Psalm 95:1–6, AMP)

SIX: PRAYER

Worship and praise is our gift to God. It's the one thing that we do not receive from him. It is doing what God cannot do for himself. Worship and praise is a sign of love and trust.

When we do something, we want to receive praise, and that will encourage us to do more. When all else has failed, praise and worship is the trump card. When we believe God for the extraordinary, we worship. When we cry out for mercy, we worship. When unbelief wants to creep in, we worship.

Worship transforms our hearts—and as we worship, his presence convicts us of sin. We cannot be a worshiper and a sinner at the same time, because worship makes his glory to reflect upon us. We are as good as the company we keep, so if we worship we will be like him who we spend time with.

Seven
DELIVERANCE

When it comes to talk of deliverance, many think the word refers to the casting out of demons. But deliverance is more than just casting out of devils. Deliverance starts with a life that is translated from the kingdom of darkness to the kingdom of light. Colossians 1:13 says, *"Who hath delivered us from the power of darkness, and hath translated us into the kingdom of his dear Son…"* (KJV)

Deliverance is about maintaining your freedom in Christ. John 8:35–36 says, *"A slave is not a permanent member of the family, but a son is part of it forever. So if the Son sets you free, you are truly free"* (NLT).

Deliverance is the renewal of the mind and crucifying the flesh. 2 Corinthians 10:4–5 reads,

> *The weapons of our warfare are not physical [weapons of flesh and blood]. Our weapons are divinely powerful for the destruction of fortresses. We are destroying sophisticated arguments and every exalted and proud thing that sets itself up against the [true] knowledge of God, and we are taking every thought and purpose captive to the obedience of Christ…* (AMP)

The major warfare we wage with the enemy is first from within, and then without. Our minds, meditations, and thoughts should be aligned with the word of God. The more we study and meditate on the word of God, the more we become like Christ. The more we become like Christ, the more the devil's sphere of influence in our lives will crumble. Our thoughts become Christ's thoughts and the flesh loses its dominion and control over us.

The Bible says that as a man *"thinketh in his heart, so is he"* (Proverbs 23:7, KJV). As we begin to think like Christ, we become Christ-like. That is what it's like to be a true Christian. We attract light when we are full of

Christ, because in him there is no darkness. Where light shines, darkness hides and demons tremble. That is the most effective spiritual warfare.

When we open the hedge of protection through sin, we must seek prayers and cast out devils. After the evil spirits are cast out, we can continue to feed our spirits with the word of God.

The more we feed our spirit man with the word of God, the more the Holy Spirit is activated in us. The Holy Spirit only understands the word of God, which is his native language. As our spirit matures, it dominates the body and soul (flesh). We cease to walk in our own passions and feelings and become spiritual beings in earthly bodies under the authority and power of the Holy Spirit.

No devil will possess or influence us if we submit to the holy spirit. James 4:7 says, *"So humble yourselves before God. Resist the devil, and he will flee from you"* (NLT). For us to live in total victory, every area of our lives should be submitted to God.

Eight
SELECTING A LOCAL CHURCH

Jesus is the head of the church, and the church is his body. I have seen a man with no legs, and I have seen a man with no hands, but I have not seen a man without a head walking down the street. Without preaching and exalting Jesus, there is no church.

We must be kingdom-minded and not just think of ourselves as church members. We have not been called to remain within the four walls of the church building; we have been called to influence the world. We have been called to bring the kingdom of God to human hearts. We are not powerful or useful to the kingdom if our salvation does not impact the next person.

> *Not forsaking the assembling of ourselves together, as the manner of some is; but exhorting one another: and so much the more, as ye see the day approaching.* (Hebrews 10:25, KJV)

We should fellowship with other Christians, for iron sharpens iron. It is wise to look for a Bible-believing church that emphasizes what Christ did on the cross, especially the epistles. Most fake preachers preach only from the Old Testament, which has led many people astray while in "church."

Look for a church that teaches prayer and Bible study. Avoid churches that lead you only to the man of God as your solution. Run from them. Avoid churches that always ask you to sow seed in order for God to do something for you. We do not pay God for anything. We bless the ministry financially for the work of God to go forward. We bless the pastors, as they have been sent by God to bless us. When it turns into spiritual abuse, run.

Appendix
Prayers and Declarations

- Father, let your glory and love overshadow us during this season, in Jesus's name. Teach us to be united in the Spirit, in Jesus's name.
- Lord, we receive the spirit of the eagle. We shall not be weary. We shall not faint. Lord, renew our strength every morning.
- Unstoppable fire of revival, begin to sweep over our families, in Jesus's name.
- Lord, set my prayer altar on fire. Set my secret place on fire, in Jesus's name.
- Lord, I pray for the gift of wisdom and discernment, in Jesus's name.

- Miracles, signs, and wonders, begin to manifest in my life, in the name of Jesus.
- Lord, give me the hunger to pray and study the word, in the name of Jesus.
- Anointing to set captives free, come upon my life, and set me free from spiritual bondages.
- Holy Spirit, you are my helper. Help me to crucify my flesh so that I can be fruitful in my Christian walk.
- Lord, take up residence and dwell in my life, in Jesus's name.

www.ingramcontent.com/pod-product-compliance
Lightning Source LLC
Chambersburg PA
CBHW061258040426
42444CB00010B/2417